The Cabrillo National Monument
The George Washington Carver National Monument
The Jefferson Memorial
The Lincoln Memorial
Mesa Verde National Park

Mount Rushmore
The Statue of Liberty
The Vietnam Veterans Memorial
The Washington Monument
The White House

AMERICA'S TOP
10
NATIONAL MONUMENTS

By
Tanya Lee Stone

Published by Blackbirch Press, Inc.
260 Amity Road
Woodbridge, CT 06525

©1998 Blackbirch Press, Inc.
First Edition

Printed in the USA

10 9 8 7 6 5 4 3

Library of Congress Cataloging-in-Publication Data

Stone, Tanya Lee.
    America's top 10 national monuments / by Tanya Lee Stone. — 1st ed.
        p. cm.—(America's top 10)
    Includes bibliographical references and index.
    Summary: Provides information about ten famous national monuments: the White House, Washington Monument, Statue of Liberty, Mesa Verde National Park, Mount Rushmore, Cabrillo National Monument, Lincoln Memorial, George Washington Carver National Monument, Jefferson Memorial, and Vietnam Veterans Memorial.
    ISBN 1-56711-194-7 (lib. bdg. : alk. paper)
    1. National monuments—United States—Miscellanea—Juvenile literature. [1. National Monuments.] I. Title. II. Series.
E159.S798   1998
973—dc21   96–52711
                                                                      CIP
                                                                      AC

B L A C K B I R C H   P R E S S ,   I N C.
W O O D B R I D G E ,   C O N N E C T I C U T

AMERICA'S TOP

10

NATIONAL MONUMENTS

OR ID

NV UT

CA

Pacific Ocean

Cabrillo
National
Monument

AZ

MEXICO

The Cabrillo National Monument

More than a million people visit the Cabrillo National Monument each year. Many of them come to catch a glimpse of the 2,000 gray whales that migrate past this location along the California coast between December and February. There is also an unusual tidal pool at this site, with a unique and rich variety of animal and plant species.

The Cabrillo National Monument was established in 1913 on Point Loma, at the entrance to present-day San Diego Bay. Point Loma was first discovered by the Portuguese explorer Juan Rodriguez Cabrillo, who anchored his ship near the spot. He was the first explorer to travel to the west coast of what is now the United States and is credited with discovering California in 1542, on September 28.

By the 1850s, there were so many boats traveling in this area that a lighthouse was built on Point Loma, 422 feet above the sea. It operated until 1891, when a new lighthouse was built on lower land so its light could shine under the fog. The original lighthouse is a favorite spot for visitors.

At the monument's visitors center there is a popular museum where visitors can watch a movie that tells the story of Juan Rodriguez Cabrillo. There is also a scenic overlook and a 14-foot-high statue of the Portuguese explorer. The statue is a replica of one created by the sculptor Alvaro DeBree in 1939. (The original statue was severely worn by the weather.) Each September, during the Cabrillo Festival, a re-enactment of Cabrillo's arrival at Point Loma is performed.

Location: San Diego, California
Size: 144 acres
Number of visitors: More than 1 million per year
Established: 1913
Height of statue: 14 feet
Weight of statue: 7 tons
Sculptor: Alvaro DeBree
Fun fact: Between 21,000 and 25,000 gray whales migrate through the eastern Pacific Ocean. About 10 percent are seen at the monument.

Opposite page:
The lighthouse on Point Loma is a popular stop for tourists.

AMERICA'S TOP
10
NATIONAL MONUMENTS

NE

IA

IL

MO

KS

George
Washington
Carver National
Monument

KY

OK

AR

TN

George Washington Carver National Monument

The George Washington Carver National Monument is the first national monument for an African American. It was created in 1943 to honor an African-American scientist who made many contributions to the field of agriculture. The monument is located at George Washington Carver's birthplace in Diamond, Missouri.

Carver was born a slave in the early 1860s and was raised by the Carver family, who owned him. After the Civil War, Carver left Diamond to study botany (the science of plants). In 1896, he went to Alabama to teach at the Tuskegee Institute. While at Tuskegee, Carver studied farming so that he could teach African Americans to become successful farmers and raise crops other than cotton. He discovered 325 new uses for peanuts and 118 ways to use sweet potatoes!

The idea for a monument to honor Carver came from a man named Richard Pilant. In the early 1940s, Pilant wrote over 700 letters to members of Congress urging them to establish a monument in Carver's honor. His efforts were successful and the George Washington Carver Memorial Associates was formed soon after.

The monument consists of 210 acres that were once part of the original Carver farm, where the scientist was born and lived as a child. On this land is a statue of Carver as a boy, the birthplace cabin site, an 1881 historic house, and the Carver family cemetery. Visitors to the George Washington Carver National Monument can walk along trails that lead them past all these sights.

Location: Diamond, Missouri
Size: 210 acres
Number of visitors: About 50,000 per year
Dedicated: July 14, 1953
Height of statue: 5 feet
Sculptor: Robert Amendola
Fun fact: One of the products Carver made from peanuts was instant "coffee."

Opposite page:
The statue of George Washington Carver as a boy sits on the land where Carver spent his childhood.

AMERICA'S TOP
10
NATIONAL MONUMENTS

MD

D.C.

VA

Jefferson
Memorial

Jefferson Memorial

Thomas Jefferson was the nation's third president and the main author of the Declaration of Independence. He was also one of Colonial America's strongest supporters of freedom and equality. This monument to him was started in 1938 and was dedicated 5 years later, on April 13, 1943—the 200th anniversary of Jefferson's birth. The white marble building, with its 26 columns and dome, is similar in style to Monticello, Jefferson's Virginia home. (Look at the back of a nickel to see what Monticello looks like.) Located on a bank of the Tidal Basin in Washington, D.C., the monument is especially beautiful when it is lighted at night.

Above the entrance to the memorial, is a sculpture that shows Jefferson standing with Benjamin Franklin, John Adams, Robert Livingston, and Roger Sherman. These men helped to write the Declaration of Independence. Engraved on 4 marble panels on the inner walls are quotations from the Declaration and other writings of Jefferson's. (There are 11 mistakes on these panels. If you visit, see if you can find them.) A 5-ton, 19-foot bronze statue of Jefferson stands in the memorial's center.

According to the memorial's original plans, the beautiful Japanese cherry trees that lined the Tidal Basin were to be torn down. Protestors chained themselves to these trees, and as a result, most of the trees were left standing. Each year, thousands of people visit Washington, D.C., just to see the trees in full bloom during the Cherry Blossom Festival.

Location: Washington, D.C.
Number of visitors:
   About 600,000 per year
Dedicated: April 13, 1943
Materials: White marble, black granite, and bronze
Height of statue: 19 feet
Weight of statue: 5 tons
Sculptor: Rudulph Evans
Cost: $3.2 million
Fun fact: The memorial was designed by John Russell Pope, Otto R. Eggers, and Daniel P. Higgins.

Opposite page:
The Jefferson Memorial was designed to look like Jefferson's home in Virginia.

MD

D.C.

Lincoln
Memorial

VA

...RS IN THE HEARTS ON... ...OR WHOM HE SAVED THE UN... ...E MEMORY OF ABRAHAM LINCO... ...IS ENSHRINED FOREVER

The
Lincoln Memorial

★ ★ ★ ★ ★ ★ ★ ★ ★ ★ ★ ★ ★ ★

The Lincoln Memorial is the most-visited tourist site in Washington, D.C. It was built in honor of America's 16th president, Abraham Lincoln, who guided the country through the Civil War. Since its dedication in 1922, this memorial has been a symbol of freedom. In 1963, on August 28, Martin Luther King, Jr.—a leader of the civil rights movement—gave his famous "I Have a Dream" speech at the memorial to a crowd of more than 200,000 people.

The memorial stands at the west end of the Reflecting Pool, which runs all the way to the Washington Monument. In 1867, 2 years after Lincoln was killed, Congress started making plans for the memorial's construction. The design was not completed until 1912, however, and work did not begin until 1914.

The marble building was designed to look like the Parthenon Temple in Greece. It has 36 exterior columns, which represent the 36 states in the Union at the time of Lincoln's death. Its 56 stone steps symbolize Lincoln's age when he died. In the monument's inner room is a white marble statue of Lincoln. The president's second inaugural speech and his Gettysburg Address are engraved on the walls there.

Underneath the Lincoln Memorial is a cave that contains beautiful limestone formations called stalagmites and stalactites. The stalagmites grow up from the floor, and the stalactites hang from the ceiling. These incredible cave formations developed from water dripping into the storage area underneath the structure.

Location: Washington, D.C.
Number of visitors: About 6 million per year
Dedicated: May 30, 1922
Material: White marble
Height of statue: 19 feet
Weight of statue: 900 tons
Sculptor: Daniel Chester French
Cost: Almost $3 million
Fun fact: The Lincoln Memorial is sited so that it is directly in line with the nation's Capitol and with the Washington Monument.

Opposite page:
A large, white marble statue of Lincoln looks out from the memorial's inner room.

AMERICA'S TOP

10

NATIONAL MONUMENTS

WY
NE
UT
CO
KS
Mesa Verde
National Park
AZ
NM
OK

★ ★ ★ ★ ★ ★ ★ ★ ★ ★ ★ ★ ★ ★ ★ ★ ★ ★

Mesa Verde National Park

Mesa Verde National Park is a monument to the Anasazi Indians. Sometimes called the "ancient ones," the Anasazi lived in what is now Colorado nearly 2,000 years ago. The park sits on a plateau and is home to the best-preserved cliff dwellings in the United States. The plateau was named Mesa Verde, or "green table," by Spanish explorers in the 18th century. All together, more than 4,000 prehistoric sites are preserved in the park.

The Anasazi began to settle in the caves at Mesa Verde in about A.D. 1. As time passed, they built complex structures from adobe clay and stone. Entire towns were built right into the cliffs. Many cliff houses are connected, creating "apartment buildings" several stories high. At the bases of these structures, the Anasazi built kivas, which are ceremonial chambers. Cliff Palace is the most amazing of the Anasazi dwellings. It has more than 200 rooms, 23 kivas, many storage chambers, and open-air courtyards. Scientists have not been able to discover why, but around A.D. 1300, the Anasazi abandoned their cliff homes. They resettled in what are now New Mexico and Arizona.

Mesa Verde National Park preserves all the cliff dwellings at this 52,000-acre site. Visitors can also see pottery and other artifacts made by the Anasazi. In 1978, Mesa Verde was named a World Heritage Cultural Site by the United Nations. Every year in July, there is a 3-day Indian Arts and Crafts Festival at the park.

Location: Southwestern Colorado
Size: 52,000 acres
Number of visitors: About 600,000 per year
Established: 1906
Fun fact: The black-and-white pottery produced by the Anasazi are among the finest ancient pots made in North America.

Opposite page:
Cliff Palace is a spectacular example of the ancient cliff houses built by the Anasazi Indians.

MT
ND
MN
WY
SD
★ Mount
Rushmore
NE
IA

★ ★ ★ ★ ★ ★ ★ ★ ★ ★ ★ ★ ★ ★ ★ ★ ★ ★ ★

Mount Rushmore

Mount Rushmore National Memorial, in the Black Hills of South Dakota, honors 4 of America's most popular presidents. Carved in the granite mountain cliff are the faces of George Washington, Thomas Jefferson, Abraham Lincoln, and Theodore Roosevelt. Doane Robinson had the idea for the monument in 1924. He chose Gutzon Borglum to be the sculptor, and Borglum decided whose portraits would be carved.

The first face sculpted out of the cliff was George Washington's. Jefferson's was done next, to the left of Washington's, but the sculptor had difficulty with the rock. Jefferson's entire head had to be blasted away! It was then carved to the right of Washington. Lincoln's portrait was chiseled next, followed by Roosevelt's.

During the project, workers were strapped into special chairs (called bosun chairs). With safety lines, they were then lowered down the mountain. Suspended in this way, they drilled, hammered, and chiseled the stone.

It took almost 400 workers 6½ years of actual working time to finish the project, but because of money problems, it was 14 years before the memorial was completed. In 1941, on March 6, Borglum died at the age of 74. His son Lincoln continued in his father's place, and Mount Rushmore was finished that October.

In 1991, on July 3, a formal dedication was held in honor of the memorial's 50th anniversary. Nineteen of the men who built the memorial attended the celebration.

Location: The Black Hills of South Dakota
Number of visitors: Almost 3 million per year
Dedicated: August 10, 1927
Completed: October 31, 1941
Material: Granite
Height of carvings: 60 feet
Height of mountain: 5,725 feet
Sculptor: Gutzon Borglum
Cost: About $1 million
Fun fact: More than 450,000 tons of rock were removed from the mountain.

Opposite page:
The faces of 4 of America's most popular presidents are carved into the Black Hills of South Dakota.

AMERICA'S TOP

10

NATIONAL MONUMENTS

CANADA
ME
VT
NH
NY
MA
RI
CT
PA
NJ
Statue of
Liberty
MD

The Statue of Liberty

★ ★ ★ ★ ★ ★ ★ ★ ★ ★ ★ ★ ★ ★ ★

The Statue of Liberty is one of the most famous landmarks in the world. In 1864, a Frenchman named Edouard-René Lefebvre de Laboulaye wanted to find a way to honor the friendship between France and America that began during the American Revolution. The sculptor Frédéric-Auguste Bartholdi came up with the idea for the statue and completed its first model by 1870.

Bartholdi decided to place the statue on an island in New York harbor. It had once been used by Native Americans and was called Oyster Island. The French planned to fund the statue, and the Americans agreed to pay for its pedestal.

Bartholdi built the statue in sections. The arm and the torch were ready by 1876. They were sent to Philadelphia for America's centennial (100th birthday) celebration. The statue was completed in France in August 1884.

The fundraising process for the pedestal did not go smoothly in America. In 1885, the well-known publisher, Joseph Pulitzer, promised to print in his newspaper the names of everyone who contributed to the project. In just 5 months, more than $100,000 was raised from the donations of 120,000 people.

In 1885, on June 17, the statue, packaged in separate sections, arrived in New York harbor. Once the pedestal was finished in 1886, assembly of the statue began. It took 75 workers 6 months to complete the job. One hundred years later, in 1986, a rededication ceremony was held on Liberty Island to celebrate this symbol of American freedom and independence.

Location: Liberty Island, New York harbor
Number of visitors: 3 million per year
Dedicated: October 28, 1886
Materials: Copper, iron
Height of statue alone: 151 feet
Height including pedestal: 305 feet
Weight of statue: 225 tons
Weight of pedestal: 27,000 tons
Number of steps: 154
Sculptor: Frédéric-Auguste Bartholdi
Cost: $650,000
Fun fact: There are 354 steps from the lobby to the crown of the statue.

Opposite page:
The Statue of Liberty stands as a welcome to travelers entering New York harbor.

The Vietnam Veterans Memorial

In Washington, D.C.'s Constitution Gardens, between Constitution Avenue and the Reflecting Pool, is the Vietnam Veterans Memorial. Many people feel that this monument is the most touching memorial in Washington, D.C. The monument is black granite and is shaped in a V. The 58,156 names of all the men and women who are missing from, or who lost their lives in, the Vietnam War are inscribed on the monument wall. These names are listed in the order in which these Americans were lost.

The monument originally consisted of the granite wall and a life-size bronze statue by Frederick Hart of 3 soldiers—1 white, 1 African American, and 1 Hispanic. In 1993, a sculpture by Glenna Goodacre was added, honoring the estimated 10,000 women who served.

Jan Scruggs, a Vietnam War veteran, had the idea for the new monument. A contest was held for its design, which was won by Maya Ying Lin, a 21-year-old student at Yale University. The memorial was dedicated on Veterans Day in 1982. During the 5-day ceremony, all of the names inscribed on the wall were read aloud—which took 60 hours.

The lettering on the memorial is small because Lin wanted people to get close to the wall in order to read the names. She thought this would help them to have a quieter, more personal experience. Thousands of people visit this memorial each year. Relatives and friends of people inscribed on the wall often leave flowers and letters in memory of their loved ones.

Location: The Mall, Washington, D.C.
Number of visitors: About 1.2 million per year
Dedicated: Veterans Day 1982
Material: Black granite
Shape: The letter V
Length: 492 feet
Number of names inscribed: 58,156
Number of panels: 140
Designer: Maya Ying Lin
Cost: About $7 million
Fun fact: Maya Ying Lin received only a B- from an art professor for the design of this celebrated memorial.

Opposite page:
A total of 58,156 names are listed on the Vietnam Veterans Memorial.

AMERICA'S TOP

10

NATIONAL MONUMENTS

MD

D.C.

Washington
Monument

VA

The Washington Monument

The Washington Monument, at just over 555 feet tall, is the tallest masonry (stone) structure in the world. It is also one of the world's most popular tourist attractions. The marble walls at its base are 15 feet thick and 55 feet wide. Each of the 50 flags flying along the base represents one of the states in the Union.

The huge monument was built to honor our nation's first president. Although it was originally planned in 1783, it took more than 100 years to complete. In 1833, the Washington National Monument Society was created to raise money for the project. Individual donations were limited to $1 so that every American could participate. When enough money was raised to begin, a design contest was held. It was won by an architect named Robert Mills. A time capsule was built into the cornerstone (the first stone laid in a foundation). Among the contents of the capsule were copies of the Declaration of Independence and the U.S. Constitution.

In the 1870s, after the Civil War, enough money was raised to continue construction of the monument. In 1884, on August 9, the last stone was set at a height of 500 feet. Four months later, on December 6, the pyramid section was secured on top and the Washington Monument was completed. It was dedicated on Washington's Birthday—February 21, 1885—and was opened to the public by 1888.

Today, the monument is one of the most popular attractions in Washington, D.C. On average, 25 people visit it every 5 minutes!

Location: Washington, D.C.
Number of visitors: More than 1 million per year
Dedicated: February 21, 1885
Material: Marble
Height: 555 feet, 5 inches
Weight: 90,854 tons
Shape: Obelisk
Number of steps: 898
Designer: Robert Mills
Cost: Almost $1.2 million
Fun fact: The ceremony marking the completion of the Washington Monument was held in gale-force winds.

Opposite page:
The Washington Monument is an obelisk, a design first used by the Ancient Egyptians.

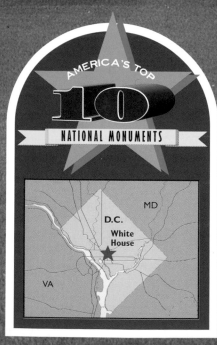

AMERICA'S TOP
10
NATIONAL MONUMENTS

MD

D.C.
White
House

VA

The
White House

The White House is one of the most important symbols of our nation. Its history dates back to 1791, when Washington, D.C., was chosen as the site for the nation's capital. In that same year, a design contest was held, which James Hoban won. The house was ready for its first occupants in 1800—the family of John Adams, the second president.

During the War of 1812, British troops set fire to the president's house. James Madison's wife, Dolley, managed to save several historic paintings before the house burned to the ground. In 1815, construction of a new house began at the same site. It was finished 5 years later. This new white building was nicknamed "The White House." In 1902, that became its official name.

There have been many important and interesting "firsts" in the White House. Our seventh president, Andrew Jackson, was the first to have indoor running water. In 1818, during President Rutherford B. Hayes's term, the first telephone was installed. In 1891, Benjamin Harrison, our 23rd president, was the first to have electric lighting installed.

In 1948, Harry Truman and his family moved out of the White House while it was being rebuilt. After 4 years of renovation, the building looked much as it does today. Since then, several First Ladies have decorated it, beginning with Jacqueline Kennedy, who founded the White House Historical Association in 1961. Among the 132 rooms are the Oval Office—where the president works— a bowling alley, movie theater, and game room.

Location: 1600 Pennsylvania Avenue, Washington, D.C.
Number of visitors: As many as 10,000 per day; about 1.5 million per year
Number of employees: About 345,000
Number of rooms: 132
Original Designer: James Hoban
Fun fact: About 50,000 calls per day are received at the White House.

Opposite page:
The White House is considered to be a symbol of the American presidency.

America's Top 10 Monuments are not necessarily the 10 "best." They pay tribute to people who have made important contributions to the nation's history and culture. Below is a list of other notable monuments and memorials.

More American Monuments & Memorials

Name, Location. *Description.*

Aztec Ruins National Monument, New Mexico. *Preserves the ruins of the Anasazi, including a multi-story pueblo with about 400 rooms.*

Booker T. Washington National Monument, Virginia. *The birthplace and boyhood home of a great African-American educator.*

Canyon de Chelly National Monument, Arizona. *Prehistoric Native American cliff dwellings.*

Clara Barton National Historic Site, Maryland. *The home of the founder of the American Red Cross.*

Confederate Monument, Georgia. *Life-size statues of Civil War generals Robert E. Lee, Stonewall Jackson, Thomas R.R. Cobb, and W.H.T. Walker.*

Devils Tower National Monument, Wyoming. *The core of an ancient volcano.*

Dinosaur National Monument, Utah and Colorado. *Thousands of dinosaur fossils are on display.*

Effigy Mounds National Monument, Iowa. *191 prehistoric Native American burial mounds.*

Eleanor Roosevelt National Historic Site, New York. *Eleanor Roosevelt's home.*

Fort Sumter National Monument, South Carolina. *The first shots of the Civil War were fired here on April 12, 1861.*

Korean War Veterans Memorial, Washington, D.C. *A tribute to the people who served in the Korean War.*

Martin Luther King, Jr. National Historic Site, Georgia. *The civil rights movement leader's birthplace, church, and gravesite.*

Muir Woods National Monument, California. *925 acres of old-growth redwood forest.*

Petroglyph National Monument, New Mexico. *More than 15,000 prehistoric and historic petroglyphs.*

USS *Arizona* Memorial, Hawaii. *Honors those who died in the attack on Pearl Harbor during World War II.*

Wright Brothers National Memorial, North Carolina. *The site where Orville and Wilbur Wright flew the first airplane.*

Glossary

agriculture The business of raising crops and livestock; farming.

archaeologist A person trained to study the way people of ancient cultures lived.

architect A person trained to design buildings and other structures.

centennial Occurring once every 100 years.

cornerstone The first stone laid in the foundation of a structure.

dedicated Opened to the public.

foundation The underlying and supporting base of a structure.

immigrant A person who comes to a country to settle there permanently.

inaugural Marking the beginning.

inscribe To write, carve, or engrave words or symbols on something.

kivas Chambers used by Native American men for ceremonial purposes.

liberty Freedom.

migrate To move seasonally from one region to another.

model A copy of something, usually built on a smaller scale.

obelisk A tall, tapering structure first built by ancient Egyptians.

pedestal An architectural support or base, as for a column or statue.

plateau An area of flat land that is raised above the surrounding area.

prehistoric The period before recorded history.

sculptor One who shapes or molds material into an artistic form.

stalactite A formation that looks like an icicle, hanging down from the ceiling of a cave.

stalagmite A formation that looks like a cone projecting from the floor of a cave.

time capsule A sealed container included in a structure, or buried by itself, that contains items of the time. The capsule is intended to be opened in the distant future.

Further Reading

Ayer, Eleanor. *I Know America: Our National Monuments*. Brookfield, CT: The Millbrook Press, 1992.

Brown, Richard, illus. *A Kid's Guide to Washington, D.C.* New York: Harcourt Brace Jovanovich, 1989.

Coerr Eleanor. *Lady With a Torch: How the Statue of Liberty Was Born*. New York: Harper and Row, 1986.

Doherty, Craig and Katherine Doherty. *Building America: Mount Rushmore*. Woodbridge, CT: Blackbirch Press, 1995.

————. *Building America: The Statue of Liberty*. Woodbridge, CT: Blackbirch Press, 1997.

————. *Building America: The Washington Monument*. Woodbridge, CT: Blackbirch Press, 1995.

Glassman, Bruce. *New York*. Woodbridge, CT: Blackbirch Press, 1991.

Kent, Deborah. *America the Beautiful: Colorado*. Chicago: Childrens Press, 1989.

————. *America the Beautiful: Washington, D.C.* Chicago: Childrens Press, 1991.

Shapiro, M.J. *How They Built the Statue of Liberty*. New York: Random House, 1994.

Where to Get On-Line Information

The Cabrillo National Monument
http://www.llbean.com/parksearch/parks/15040GD10027GD.html

The George Washington Carver National Monument
http://www.coax.net/people/LWF/carver.htm

The Jefferson Memorial http://www.nps.gov/thje/index2.htm

The Lincoln Memorial http://www.nps.gov/linc/index2.htm

Mesa Verde National Park http://www.nps.gov/meve

Mount Rushmore http://www.state.sd.us/state/executive/tourism/rushmore/rushmore.htm

The Statue of Liberty http://www.fieldtrip.com/ny/23637620.htm

The Vietnam Veterans Memorial http://www.nps.gov/vive/index.htm

The Washington Monument http://www.nps.gov/wamo/index2.htm

The White House http://www.whitehouse.gov

Index

Photo Credits

Cover (Washington Monument): ©Blackbirch Press, Inc.; Cover (Statue of Liberty and Mesa Verde National Park) and page 10: PhotoDisc, Inc.; cover and page 2: ©Cecil W. Stoughton/National Park Service; cover and page 4: Permission granted by the Missouri Division of Tourism; cover and page 6: ©William Clark/National Park Service; cover and pages 8, 14, 16, 18, 20: ©Blackbirch Press, Inc.; cover and page 12: Photo by South Dakota Tourism